Great-g
Danci

Helen Dunmore

Illustrated by Sam Thompson

CAMBRIDGE
UNIVERSITY PRESS

Cambridge Reading

General Editors
Richard Brown and Kate Ruttle

Consultant Editor
Jean Glasberg

PUBLISHED BY THE PRESS SYNDICATE OF THE UNIVERSITY OF CAMBRIDGE
The Pitt Building, Trumpington Street, Cambridge CB2 1RP, United Kingdom

CAMBRIDGE UNIVERSITY PRESS
The Edinburgh Building, Cambridge CB2 2RU, United Kingdom
40 West 20th Street, New York, NY 10011-4211, USA
10 Stamford Road, Oakleigh, Melbourne 3166, Australia

Text © Helen Dunmore 1998
Cover and text illustrations © Sam Thompson 1998

First published 1998
Reprinted 1998

Printed in the United Kingdom at the University Press, Cambridge

Typeset in Concorde

A catalogue record for this book is available from the British Library

ISBN 0 521 63744 9 paperback

Other Cambridge Reading books you may enjoy

Leaving the Island
Judith O'Neill

A True Spell and a Dangerous
Susan Price

Half of Nowhere
Richard Burns

Never Meddle with Magic Mirrors!
Kaye Umansky

Other books by Helen Dunmore you may enjoy

Clyde's Leopard

Amina's Blanket

Allie's Apples

Go Fox

Rosa coloured in the birthday card as fast as
she could. She was supposed to be drawing
a map of a Roman town, and any second now
Mrs Hayes would come round to see how
everyone was getting on. Red for the tulips,
brown and yellow for the basket. What colour
for the ribbon? Blue. Deep, glossy blue. But
Rosa hadn't got a dark-blue pencil.

"Charmaine!" she whispered.

"What?"

"Can I borrow your dark blue?"

"What're you doing?" Charmaine twisted round. Her sharp green eyes lit on the card. "Who's that for?"

"It's a birthday card for my great-grandma," said Rosa. She knew she might as well tell Charmaine straight away, because she always found out things in the end.

"Let's have a look." Charmaine snatched up the card. "It's brilliant, Rosa!" she said in a voice as sweet as ice-cream. But Rosa knew that voice. Charmaine fixed Rosa with eyes like magnets. "Do one for me, Rosa. Go on. It's my mum's birthday next week."

That was true, Rosa knew it. Her mum and Charmaine's mum were nurses in the same hospital, and Rosa and Charmaine had gone to the same childminder, the same nursery and then the same school. Year after year, Charmaine sat next to Rosa. Rosa never had to find a partner for gym or dancing or walking up to the school field, because Charmaine was always there. Sometimes Rosa wondered what it would be like to choose someone else, but she never dared.

Charmaine's green eyes would snap and she would say horrible things to Rosa, the kind of things that only someone who knows you really well can say. Charmaine knew that Rosa was frightened of rats. Once Charmaine had said a rat had come out of the sewers and got into Rosa's garden. For two whole weeks, Rosa could not go into the garden, even though it was the hottest time of the summer and her grandma had just bought her a tent. At last she told Mum, and Mum said it wasn't true about the rat. Lots of the things that Charmaine said weren't true, but Rosa never knew which ones.

"I'll give you my Disneyland rubber if you do," said Charmaine.

"OK," said Rosa slowly, even though she didn't want the Disneyland rubber. Now Charmaine would tell her mum she'd made the card herself, when it was really Rosa.

Charmaine beamed. "Here you are. Only don't use it too much," she said, handing Rosa her glossy, dark-blue pencil. Charmaine's coloured pencils always looked brand new.

Probably because she never does any drawing, thought Rosa. She began to colour in the numerals. Red for the 9, dark blue for the 2. 'Happy Birthday, 92 today'. She shaded the colour in carefully, slowly, until it was perfect.

"Hurry up," said Charmaine, "you'll never get mine done if you go as slow as that." Out of the corner of her eye, Rosa saw Mrs Hayes stand up. She slid the birthday card under her folder and bent over her Roman map. It was quite good, but the shading was smudged where Charmaine's elbow had rubbed it.

As soon as Mrs Hayes had gone back to her desk after looking at everyone's maps, Charmaine shoved a folded piece of white drawing paper in front of Rosa. "Go on, quick!" she said, and Rosa began on the card for Charmaine.

The next day it was Great-grandma's birthday. But there wasn't going to be a birthday celebration, because Mum and Grandma were both working. Instead, she and Mum were going to bake a cake and have a birthday tea for Great-grandma on Saturday. But Rosa thought it was horrible for her great-grandma not to have anything on her proper birthday, even though she was so old she probably didn't care much about birthdays any more. Maybe Rosa could take the card round after school. Then she remembered that she'd already said she'd go to Charmaine's house after school.

Perhaps Charmaine won't mind, thought Rosa hopefully, but she knew Charmaine would. At break time, she gave Charmaine half her Milky Way. While Charmaine's mouth was full, she said quickly, "Listen, Charmaine, you know it's my great-grandma's birthday? Well, she's on her own till Grandma comes back from work, so I thought I'd take her my card after school and say happy birthday."

Charmaine swallowed the Milky Way in one gulp. "You're coming round to my house," she said. Her eyes bored into Rosa's.

"I know. But . . . but can't I come tomorrow instead?"

"Can't I come tomorrow?" imitated Charmaine in a squeaky, pathetic little voice. "I haven't *asked* you to come tomorrow. I asked you to come *today*, and you said yes, so now you've got to come."

Rosa felt herself go red. "It's only because it's her birthday."

"I know it's her *birthday*. You've already told me that about a million times. Listen, Rosa, we're going to do something really good at my house. Mum said if we were careful we could make ice-cream in her new ice-cream maker. Chocolate ice-cream."

Rosa opened her mouth. She was going to do what Charmaine wanted. It was like slipping down a slide she'd slid down hundreds of times before. It was so easy. Then she thought of the card she'd made. The red tulips, the blue ribbon. And Great-grandma sitting watching TV just as she always did, as if it wasn't her birthday at all.

"I'm sorry, Charmaine," she said, "but I think I should go and see her. She's on her own and she's really old and . . ."

Charmaine leaned forward until her face was only a few inches from Rosa's. "I know she's really old. And she's really stupid. She's a deaf, stupid old bat and I hope she dies before she has another birthday and you make another stupid birthday card for her. And you needn't think I'm going to be your friend any more, because I'm not. *And* you're never coming round to my house again." Charmaine did not shout. She never shouted. Her voice just got colder and snakier, and her fingers pinched hard into Rosa's arm. Then she gave Rosa a push and walked off.

For the rest of the day, Charmaine didn't speak to Rosa. She looked at her a lot, and giggled as if there were something funny about Rosa. When the bell rang, Rosa went to her drawer to get the birthday card for her great-grandma. It wasn't in the blue folder. It wasn't in the plastic folder where Rosa kept her school library book. It wasn't with Rosa's other drawings. The birthday card had gone. Rosa looked through everything one more time, but she knew it was no good. Charmaine had taken the card, but she would never, ever admit it. Rosa knew what would happen. In about a week, when they were friends again, when Great-grandma's birthday was over, Charmaine would find the card and say,

"Oh look, Rosa, here's your birthday card! It was in your drawer all the time. You can't have looked properly."

Rosa knelt by her drawer. Nearly everyone had gone. Only Maxine was still by the drawers, putting her homework into her bag. She gave Rosa a quick little smile. "You OK, Rosa?"

"Yeah. I've lost something, that's all."

Maxine hesitated. Then she said, "I've got gymnastics, or I'd stay and help you look."

"I didn't know you went to gymnastics," said Rosa. She'd always wanted to do gymnastics.

"It's brilliant. I've been going to the Gym Centre since the beginning of term. You ought to try it, you'd be good." Maxine did up the top of her bag. "See you tomorrow, Rosa." But she didn't walk off straight away. Instead, she said, a bit shyly, "You can come with me and watch next week if you want. See if you like it."

Maxine was nice. Rosa wondered why she'd never talked to her like this before. But then, on a normal day Rosa would have already left with Charmaine.

Great-grandma's room was dark except for the flickering light of her TV. She was sitting in her chair with her eyes closed.

"It's me! Happy birthday, Great-grandma!" shouted Rosa. It wasn't rude to shout at Great-grandma, because if you didn't she'd never hear anything. Slowly, Great-grandma opened her eyes. She pressed the remote control that lay on her knee and the TV screen went dark.

"Open the curtains, child, and let the sun in."

"It isn't sunny, Great-grandma, it's raining."

"Never mind. Rain is good for farmers," said Great-grandma. She had lived in the city for sixty years, but she still thought about farmers.

"I made you a card," said Rosa, "but it got lost. I'm really sorry."

"You tell me about it. You tell me good enough and I'll see it." Great-grandma didn't speak the same as other people, because until she was twenty and came to England she had never spoken one word of English.

"There were tulips, red tulips with beautiful, pale-green leaves, all in a basket. And I drew a dark-blue ribbon round the basket. It was really good."

"I see it now. So how come you lost such a beautiful thing?"

Rosa knelt down by Great-grandma's chair and fiddled with the remote control. "I think," she said, "I think somebody took it."

"Somebody jealous of your so beautiful drawing," said Great-grandma. Rosa was glad Charmaine wasn't there to laugh at the way Great-grandma talked.

"Yes," she said.

"Hmm," said Great-grandma. Her little, bony hand pushed the hair back from Rosa's forehead and she looked into Rosa's face. Rosa looked back. People always said that Rosa looked like her great-grandma, but Rosa could never believe it. Great-grandma was so old. Her face was cracked all over with lines, like a piece of dried-up earth. But her bright black eyes were not so old. Maybe those eyes were a little bit like the eyes Rosa saw in the mirror.

"Did you ever do gymnastics," asked Rosa, "when you were young?"

"Gymnastics! Never. It would have been forbidden."

"Why?"

"Many things were forbidden when I was young, especially for us girls. I will tell you something. When I was a girl I had a new blue dress, a beautiful dress, the best I ever had. My mother made it for me because she knew I wanted a dancing dress. I wanted to go to the dance in our village. I wanted that more than I ever wanted anything. Just to go and dance with my friends. I begged my father to let me go, but he took my dress and put it under his mattress and lay on his bed on top of it and he went to sleep. And I had no other dress. Already, I could hear the music from the hall where the dance had begun."

"So you couldn't go," said Rosa.

"Oh, couldn't I?" Rosa looked at Great-grandma's face. She was smiling, her dark, sharp eyes snapping in her wrinkled face. "I'll tell you the rest of the story," she said.

"When my father was asleep and snoring, my mother put her finger on her lips and we tiptoed into the bedroom. It was dark. My mother stood on one side of the bed and I stood on the other. Then both together we

lifted the mattress a tiny, tiny bit and my
mother pulled out the dress. And I went
dancing in it. I knew my father would beat me
if he found out, but he never did. He snored
all night and we put the dress back under the
mattress when I came home."

Rosa thought of the big, angry father, snoring on the mattress. "You must have been frightened when you went into his room," she said.

"Oh yes, I was frightened. My heart thumped so loud I was sure he would hear it and wake up. And my mother was frightened too. But sometimes you have to be brave, or you never do anything in your life."

"I'll make you another card, Great-grandma," promised Rosa. "It'll be even better this time. I'll bring it tomorrow."

But Great-grandma did not seem to hear. She was getting tired. She smiled at Rosa, then she switched on the TV and shut her eyes again. Rosa tiptoed out of the room. Mum would be waiting for her at home.

The next morning, Rosa was hanging up her jacket in the school cloakroom when Charmaine came in.

"That chocolate ice-cream I made last night," said Charmaine, hanging her jacket next to Rosa's, "it was *delicious*. It was the best ice-cream I've ever tasted."

"Good," said Rosa.

"What's the matter with *you*?" asked Charmaine. "It was only a joke, what I said about your great-grandma. Can't you take a joke?"

Rosa fumbled in the pocket of her jacket, pretending she was looking for something. Her heart was banging. She was afraid that if she said anything her voice would be squeaky and pathetic, like the voice Charmaine imitated. Charmaine was staring at her.

Rosa took a handkerchief out of her jacket
pocket, as if that had been what she'd been
looking for. Then, just as if nothing had
happened, Charmaine said, "You can come to
my house after school if you want. Since you
didn't come yesterday."

Rosa took a deep breath. "I'm sorry," she said. "I'm going to my great-grandma's again. I have to take her another birthday card. The one I made yesterday got lost."

"You don't have to," said Charmaine. Her voice was sweet and friendly. She knows where my birthday card is, Rosa told herself.

Charmaine smiled confidently, as if she already knew that Rosa would do as she said. "You don't have to go round to your great-grandma's. It's not her birthday any more."

Suddenly Rosa did not see Charmaine. She saw her great-grandma, and her great-great-grandma, standing on each side of a mattress where a big, heavy man was snoring. She saw them lift up the mattress, and pull out her great-grandma's dancing dress. Sometimes, said her great-grandma's voice, you have to be brave, or you never do anything in your life. Rosa took another deep breath. She seemed to see her great-grandma's eyes watching her. Great-grandma's eyes were young, though the rest of her was old. She was waiting to see what Rosa would do.

"I can't come to your house today, Charmaine," said Rosa. Then she turned and walked out of the cloakroom. Her back felt as if it was burning where Charmaine stared after her.

In the classroom there was Maxine, taking stuff out of her bag.

"How was gymnastics?" asked Rosa.

"It was great. Are you going to come next week?"

"Yes," said Rosa, "I think I will. Thanks, Maxine." Then she went to her drawer, and took out her pencils to begin a new birthday card for her great-grandma.